D1462435

You Can Go Jump

A Follett Beginning-To-Read Book
Level One

You Can Go Jump

Valjean McLenighan
illustrated by Jared D. Lee

FOLLETT PUBLISHING COMPANY
Chicago

International Standard Book Number: 0-695-30744-4 Paper Binding

International Standard Book Number: 0-695-40744-9 Titan Binding

123456789/828180797877

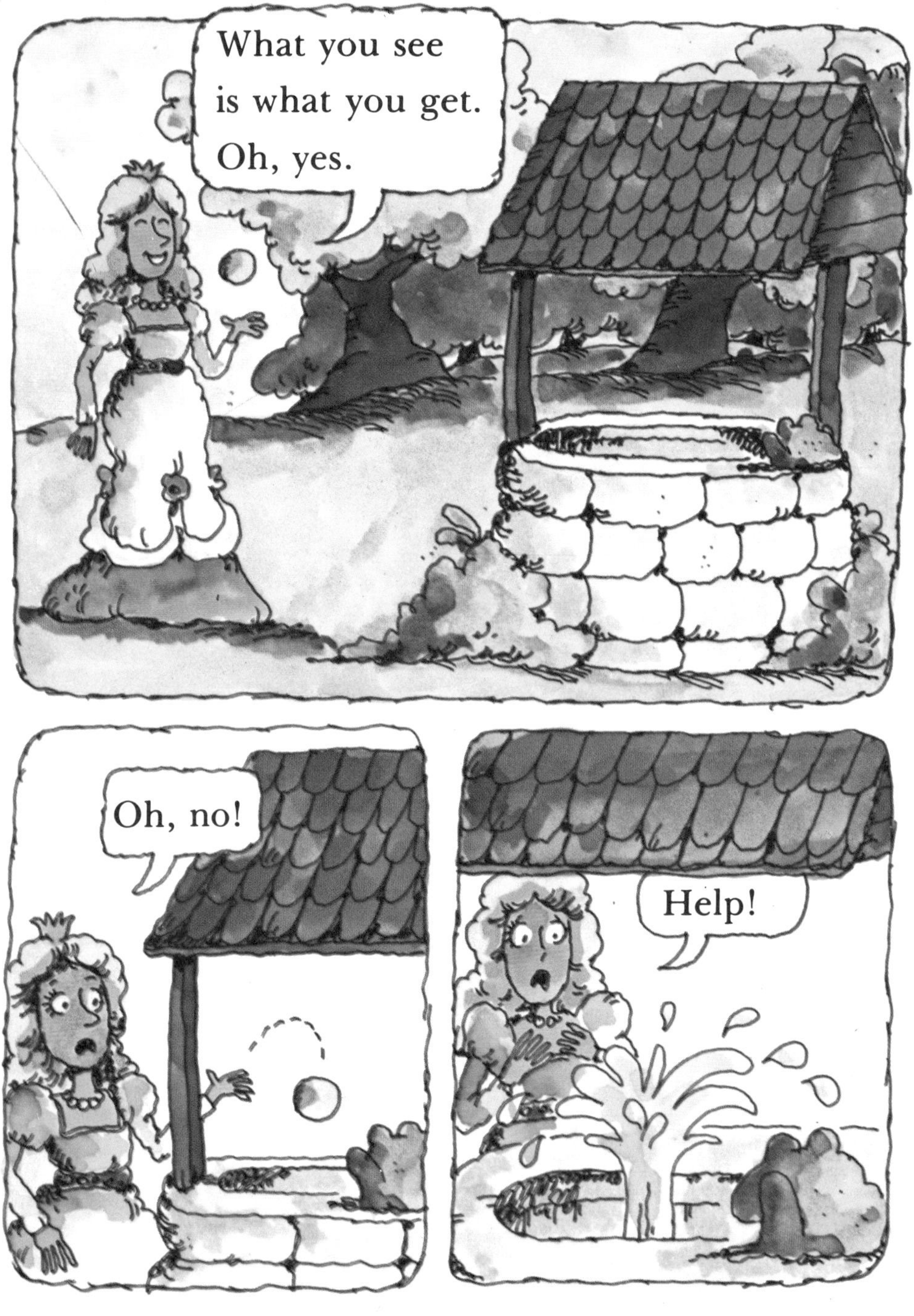
What you see
is what you get.
Oh, yes.
Oh, no!
Help!

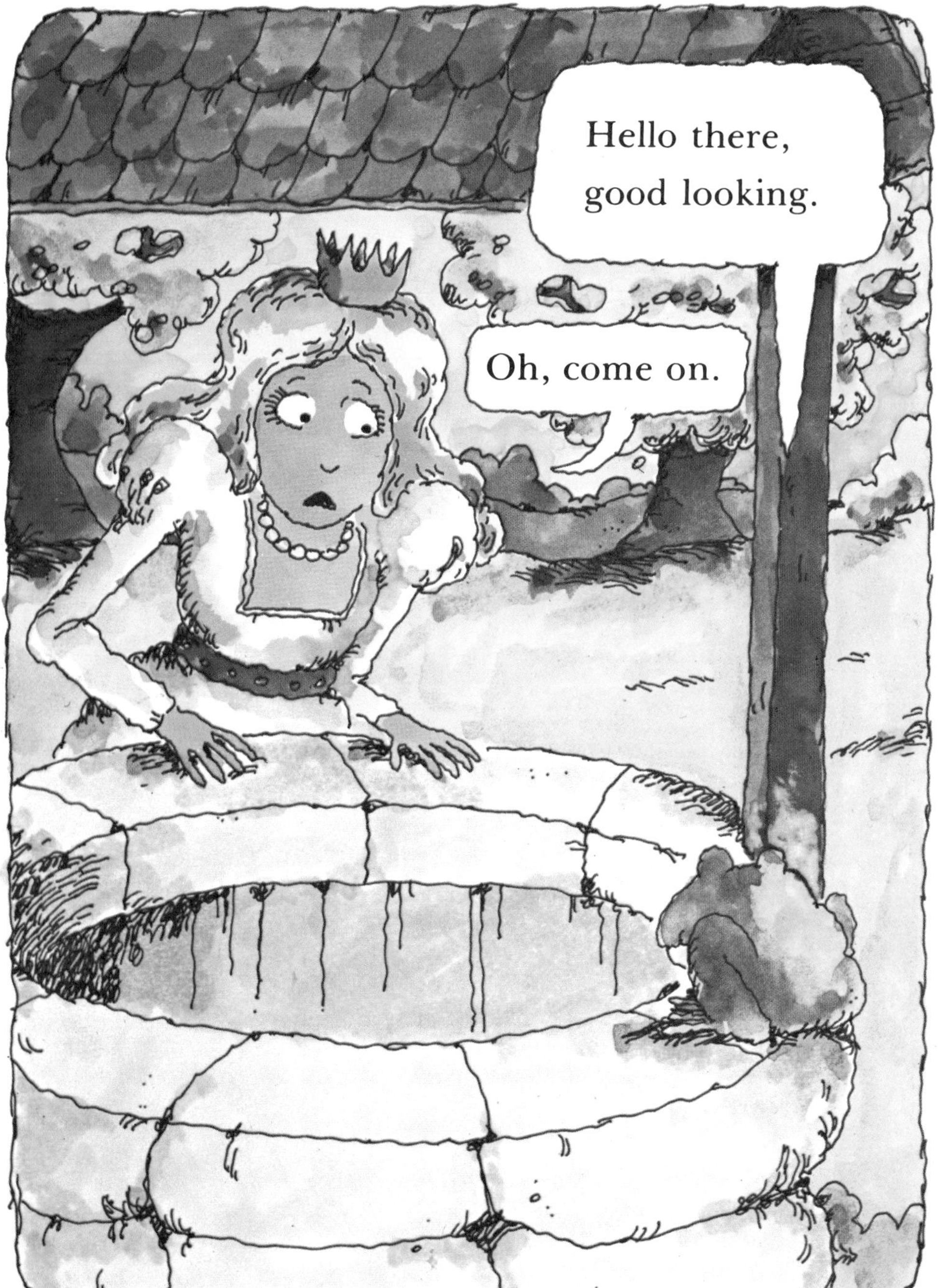
Hello there, good looking.
Oh, come on.

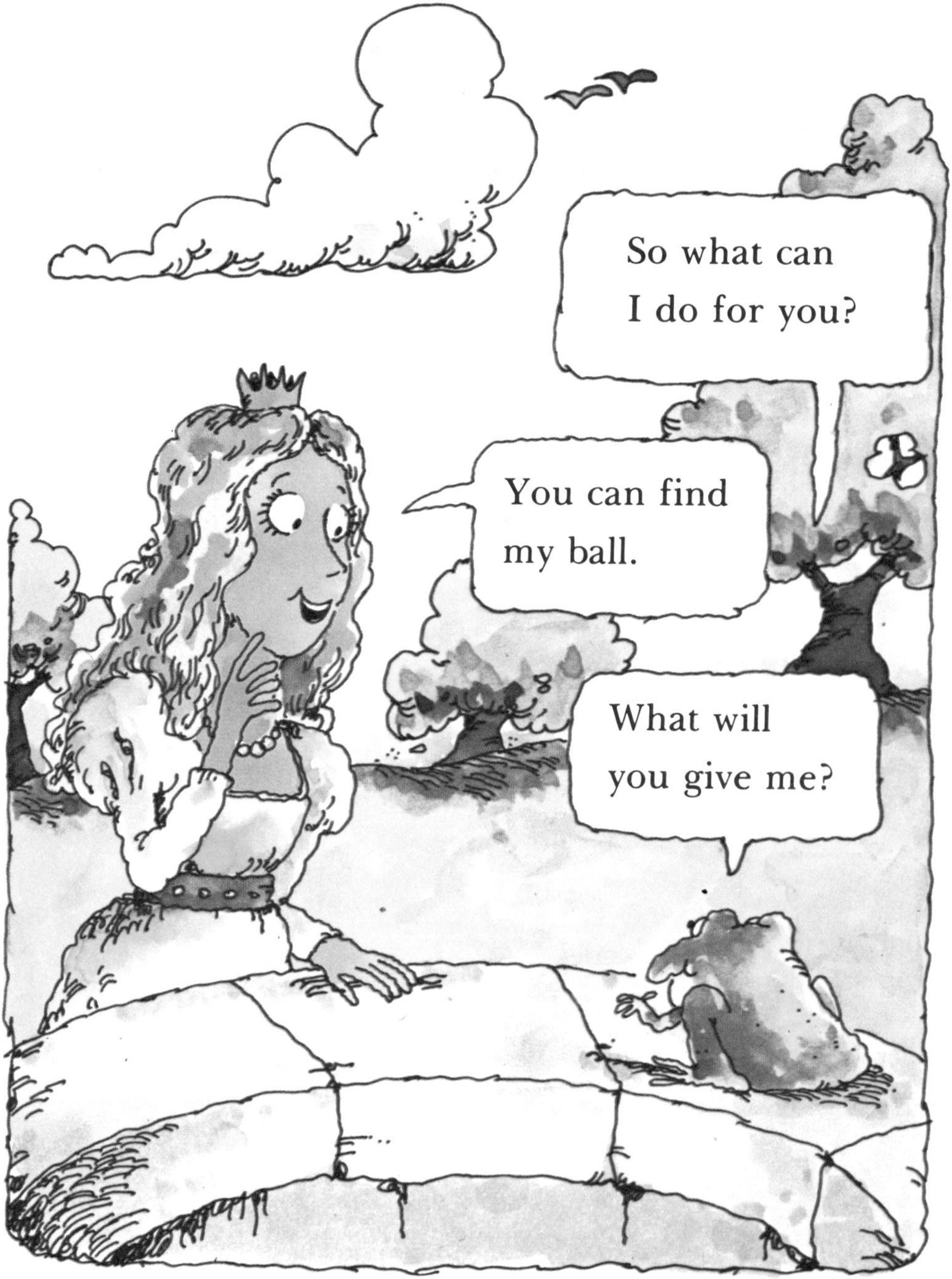
So what can I do for you?
You can find my ball.
What will you give me?

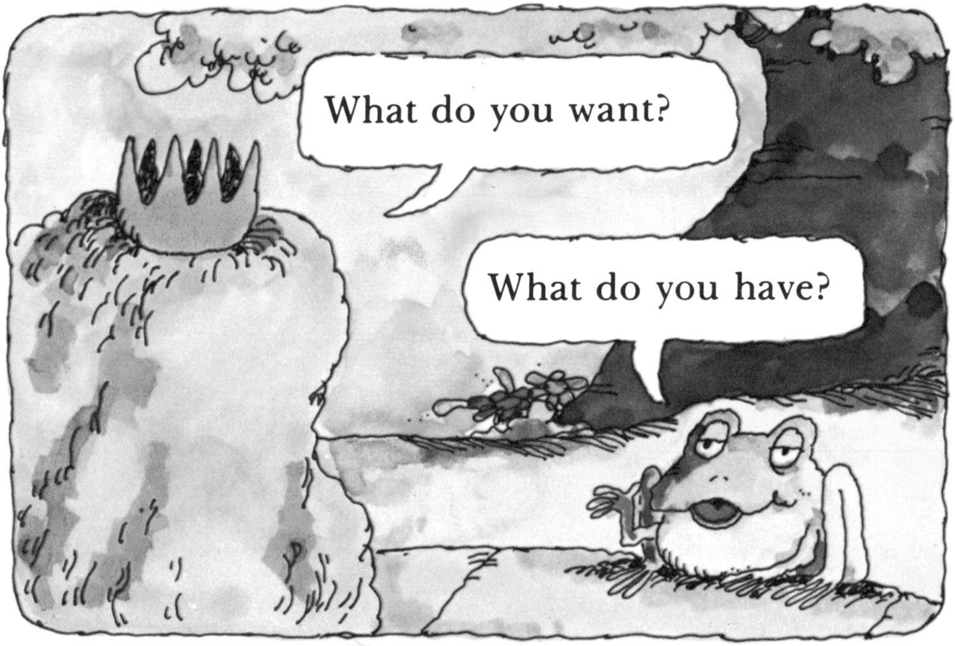
What do you want?
What do you have?

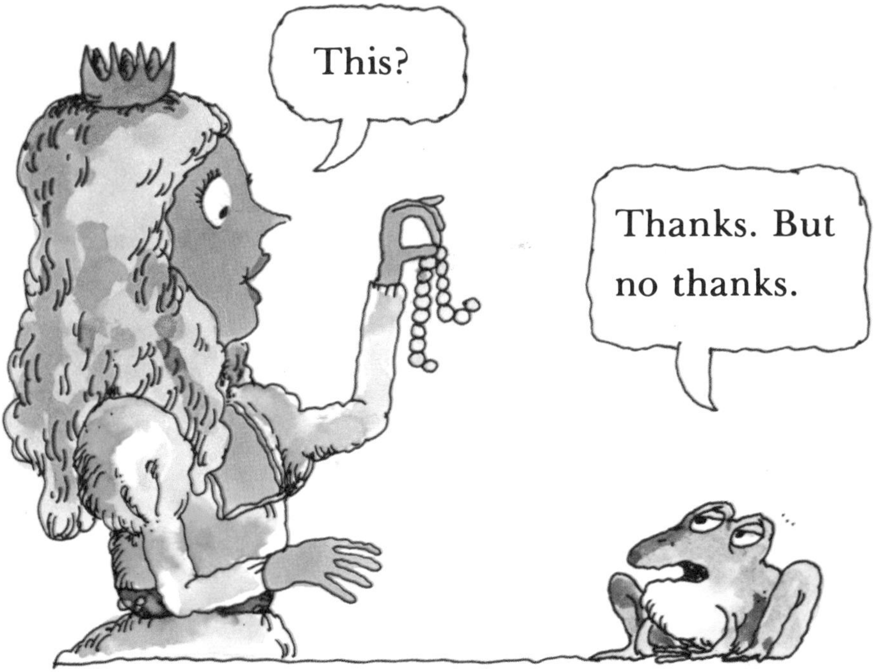
This?
Thanks. But no thanks.

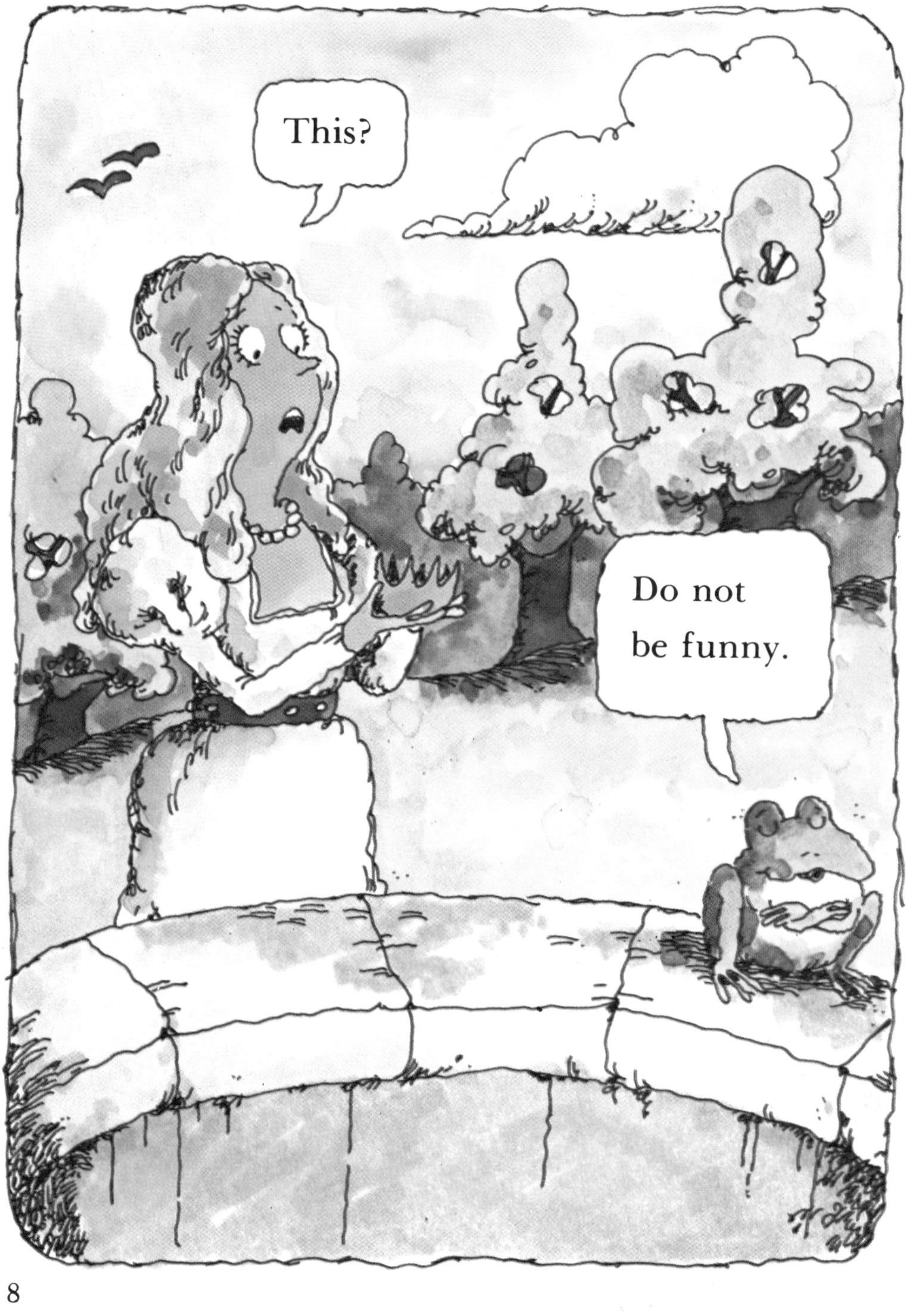
This?
Do not
be funny.

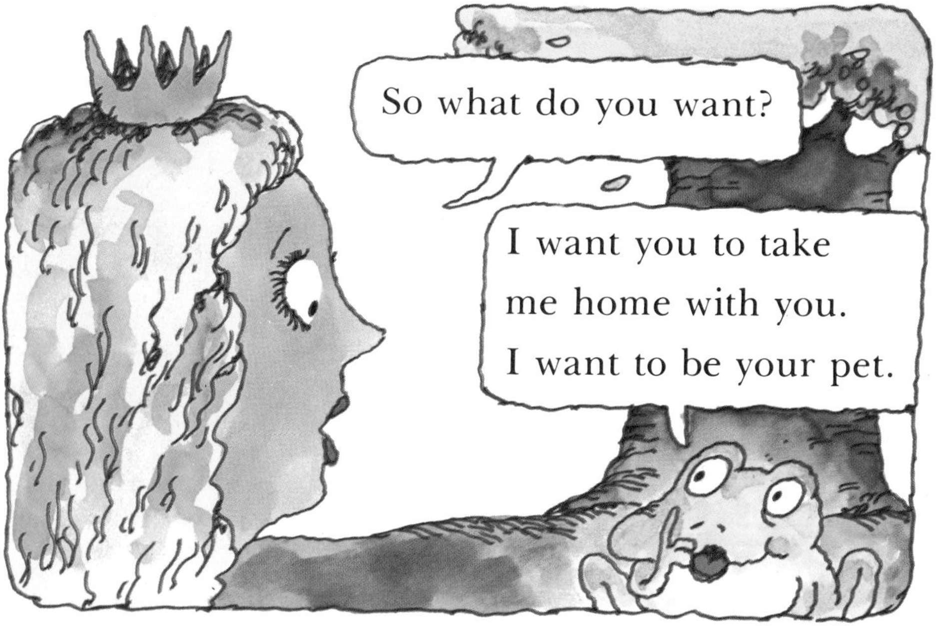
So what do you want?
I want you to take me home with you. I want to be your pet.

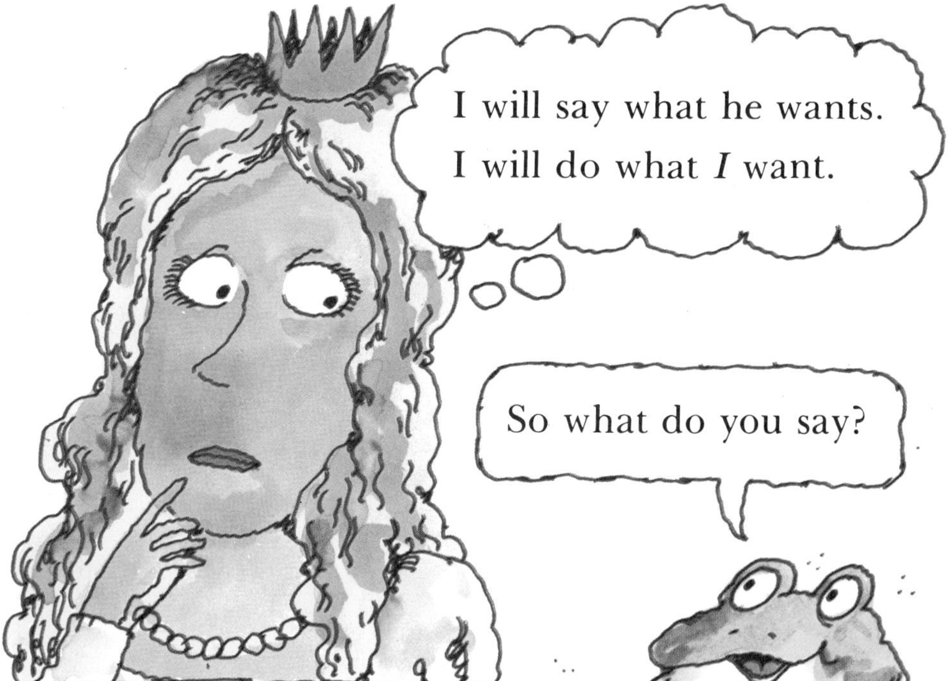
I will say what he wants. I will do what *I* want.
So what do you say?

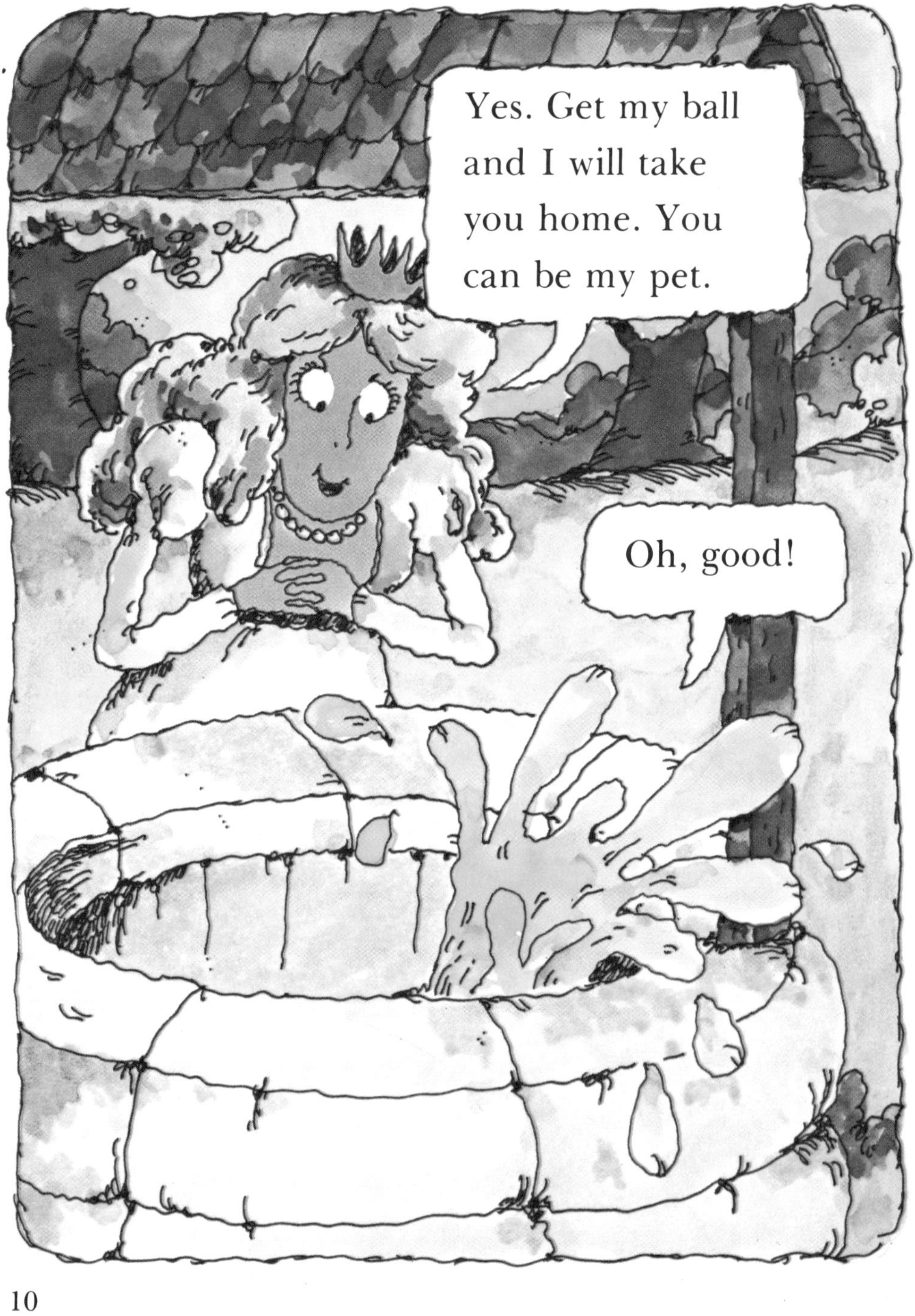
Yes. Get my ball and I will take you home. You can be my pet.
Oh, good!

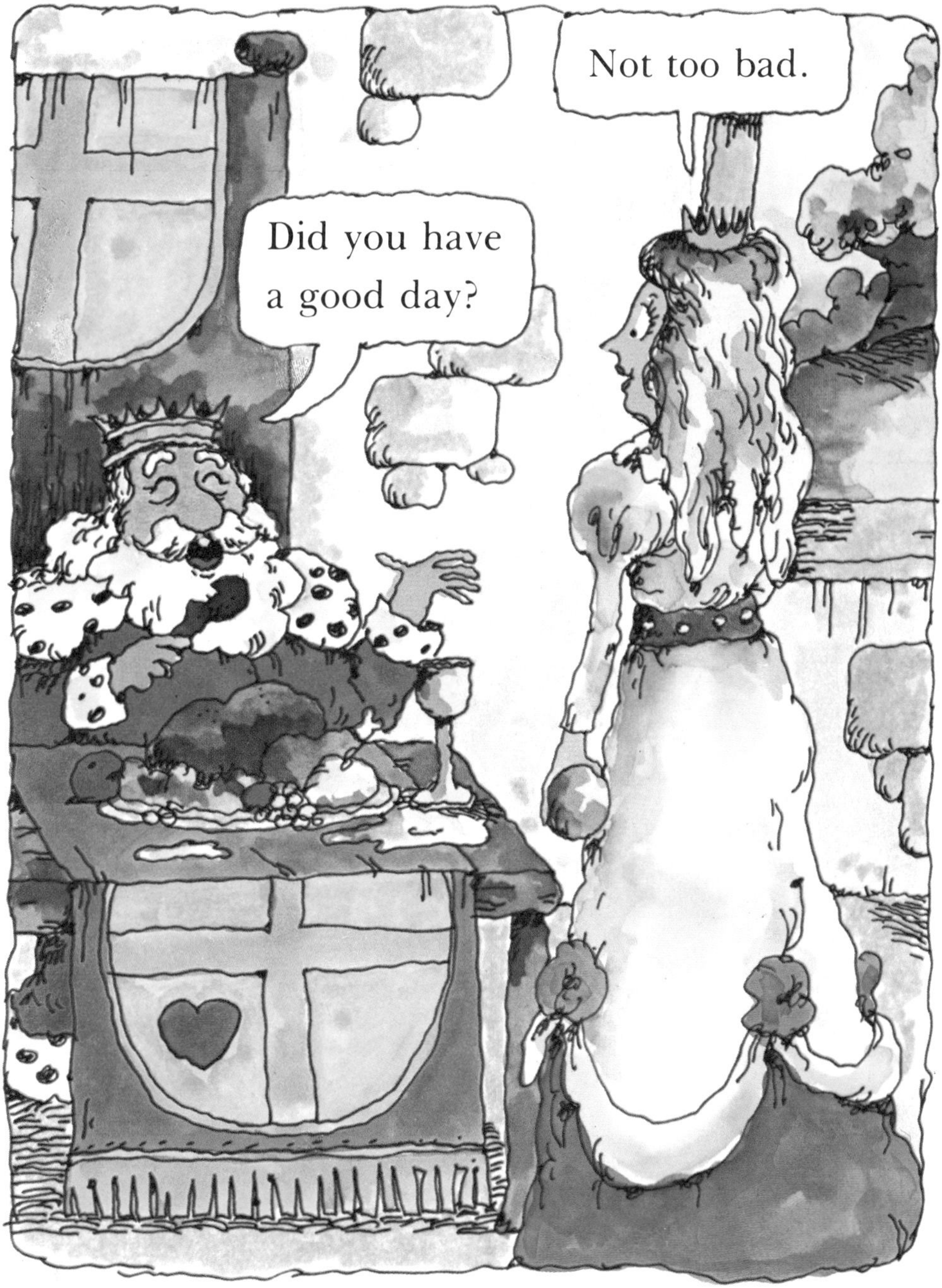
Not too bad.
Did you have a good day?

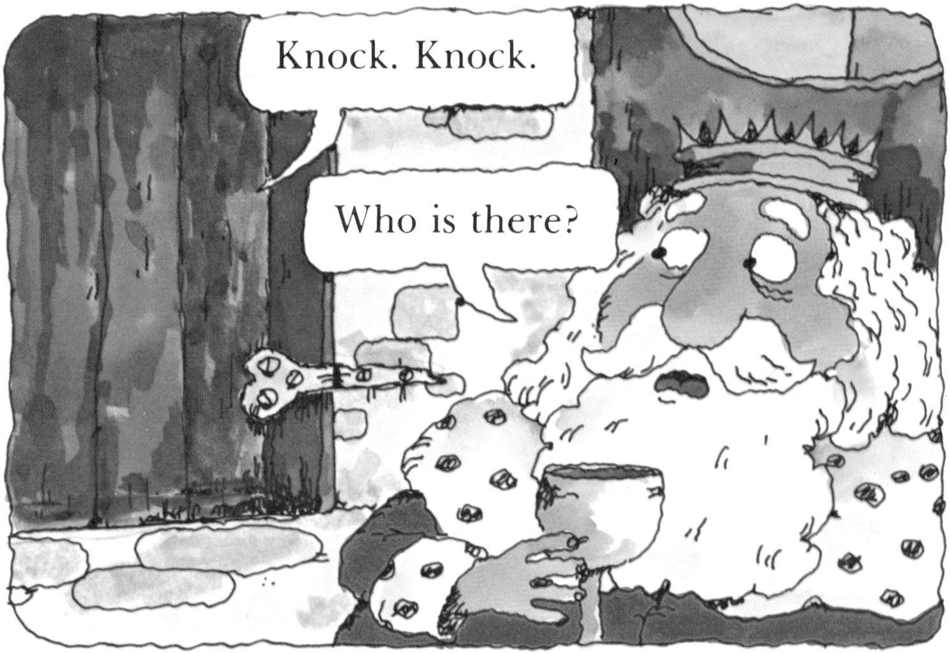
Knock. Knock.
Who is there?

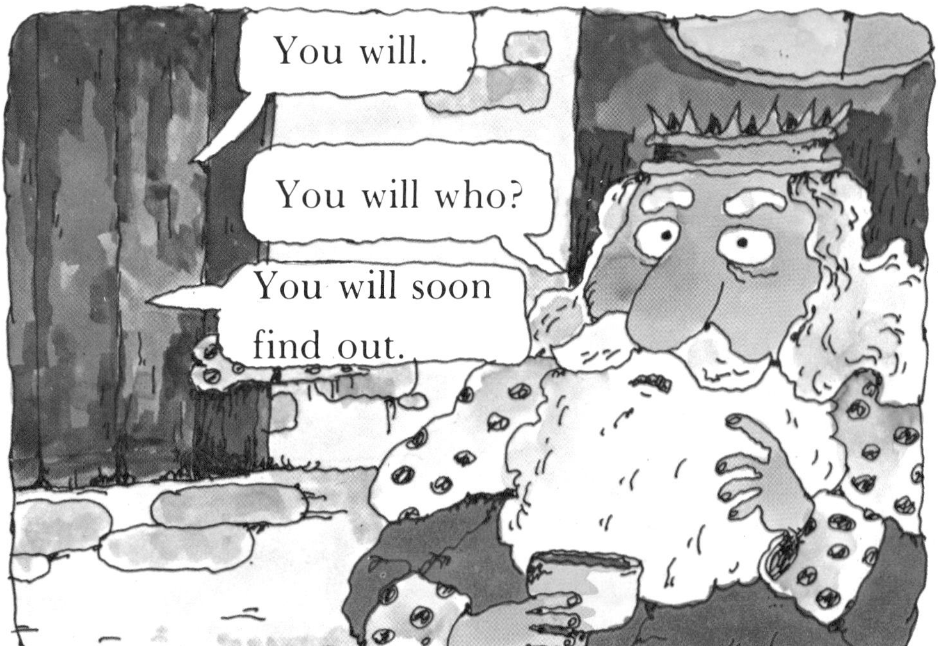
You will.
You will who?
You will soon find out.

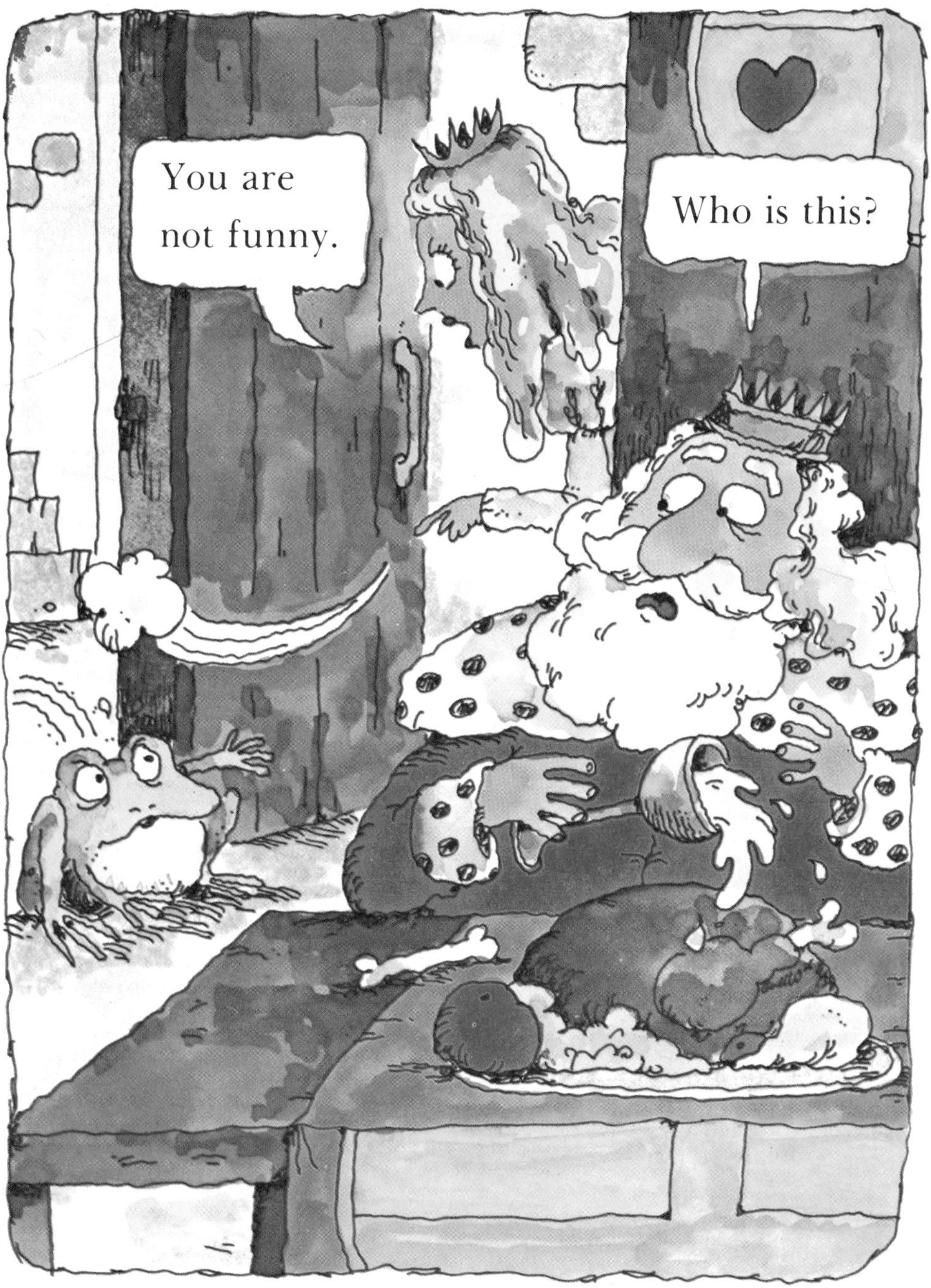
You are
not funny.
Who is this?

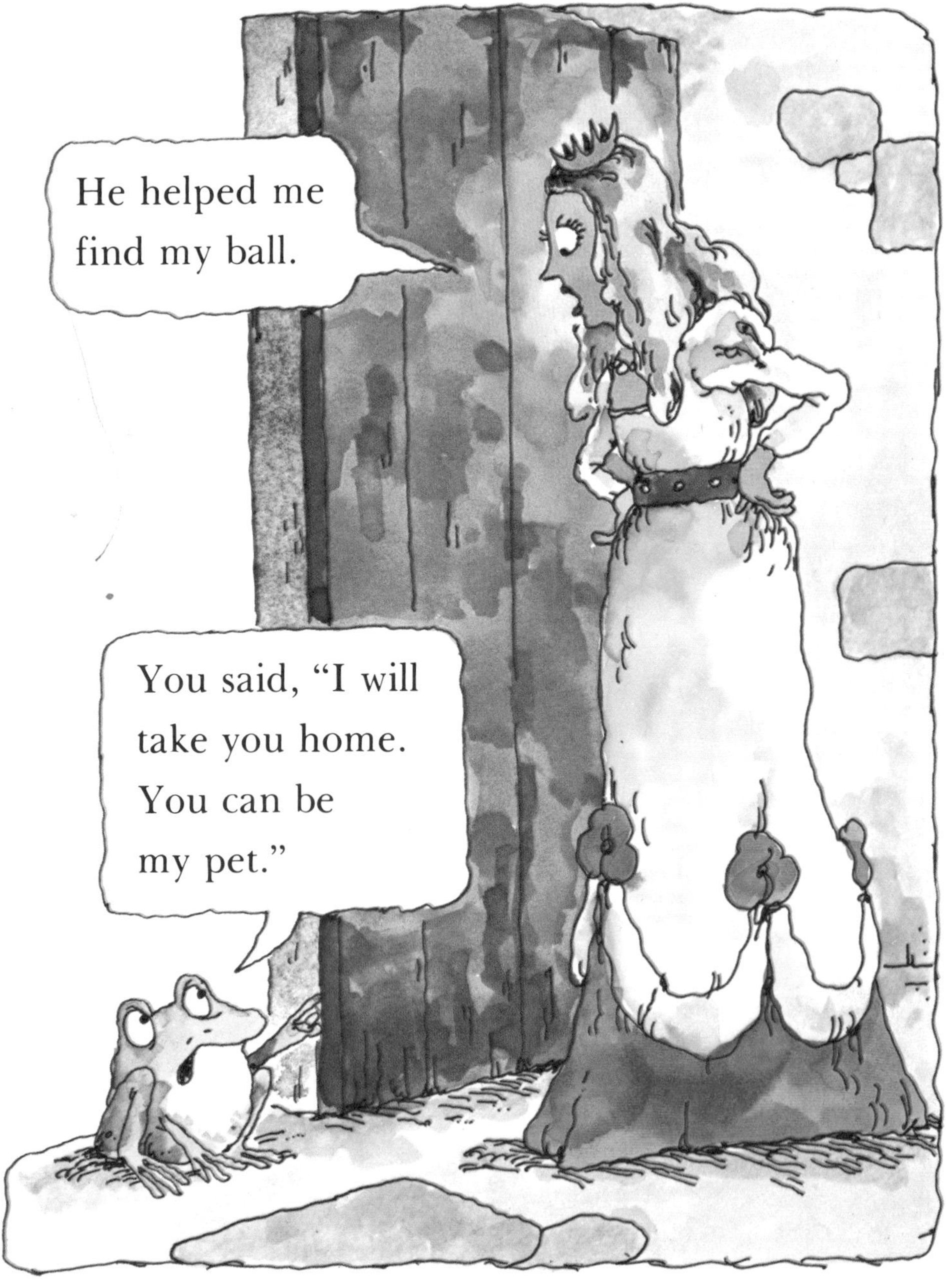
He helped me find my ball.
You said, "I will take you home. You can be my pet."

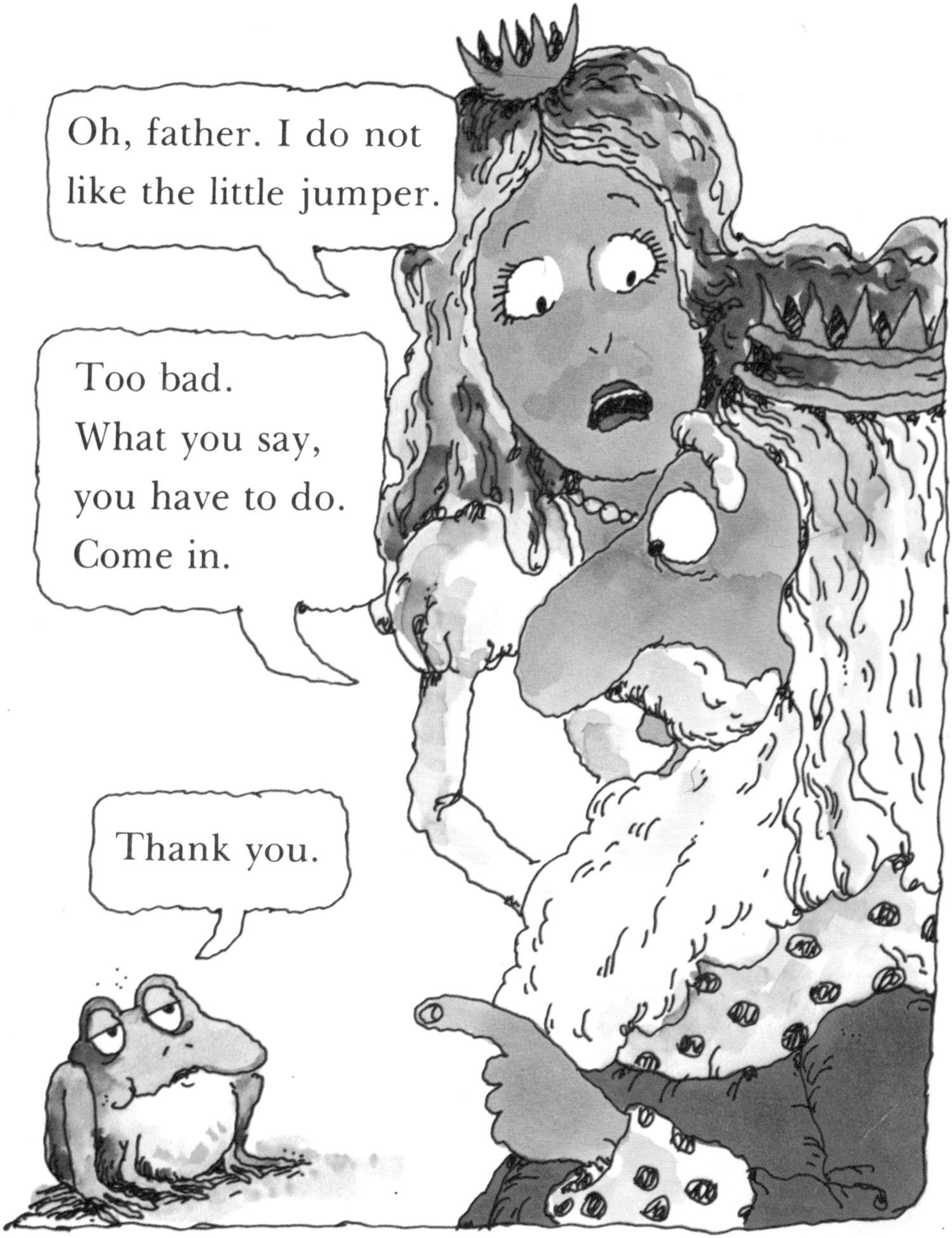
Oh, father. I do not like the little jumper.
Too bad. What you say, you have to do. Come in.
Thank you.

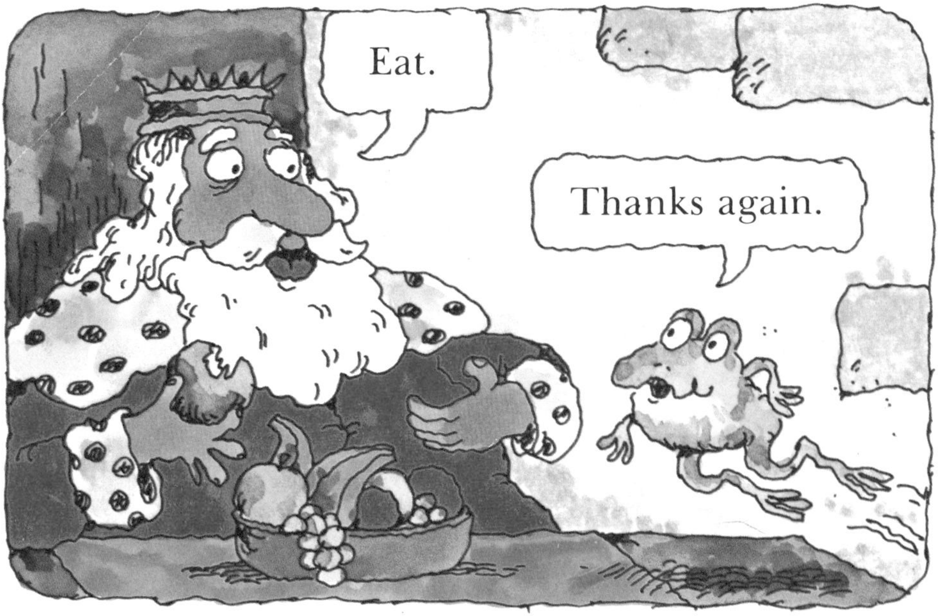
Eat.
Thanks again.

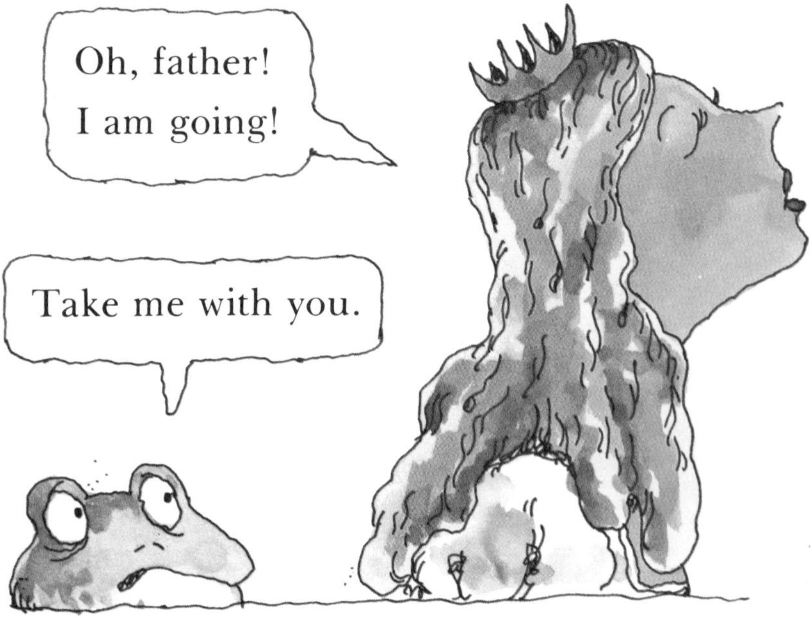
Oh, father! I am going!
Take me with you.

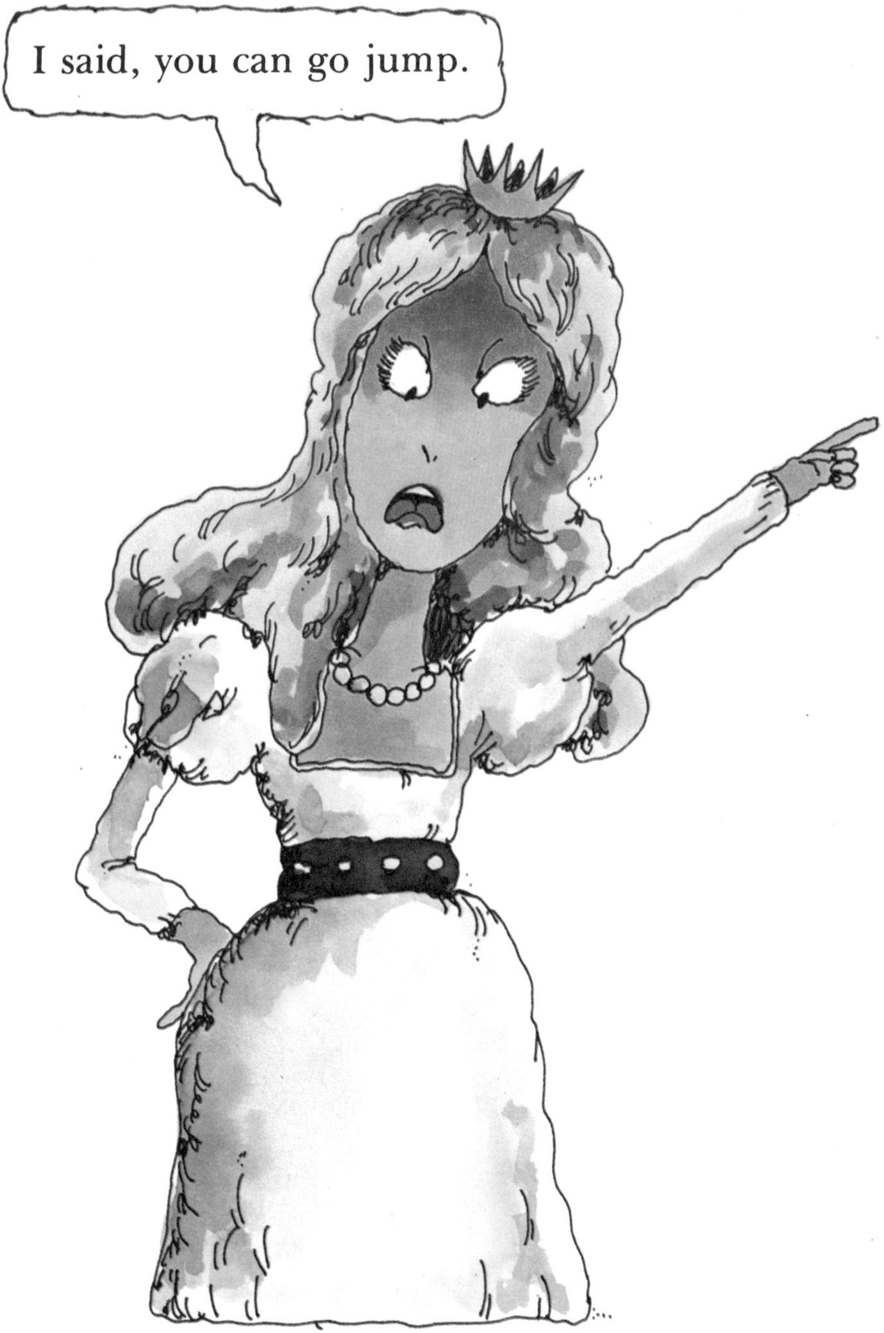
I said, you can go jump.

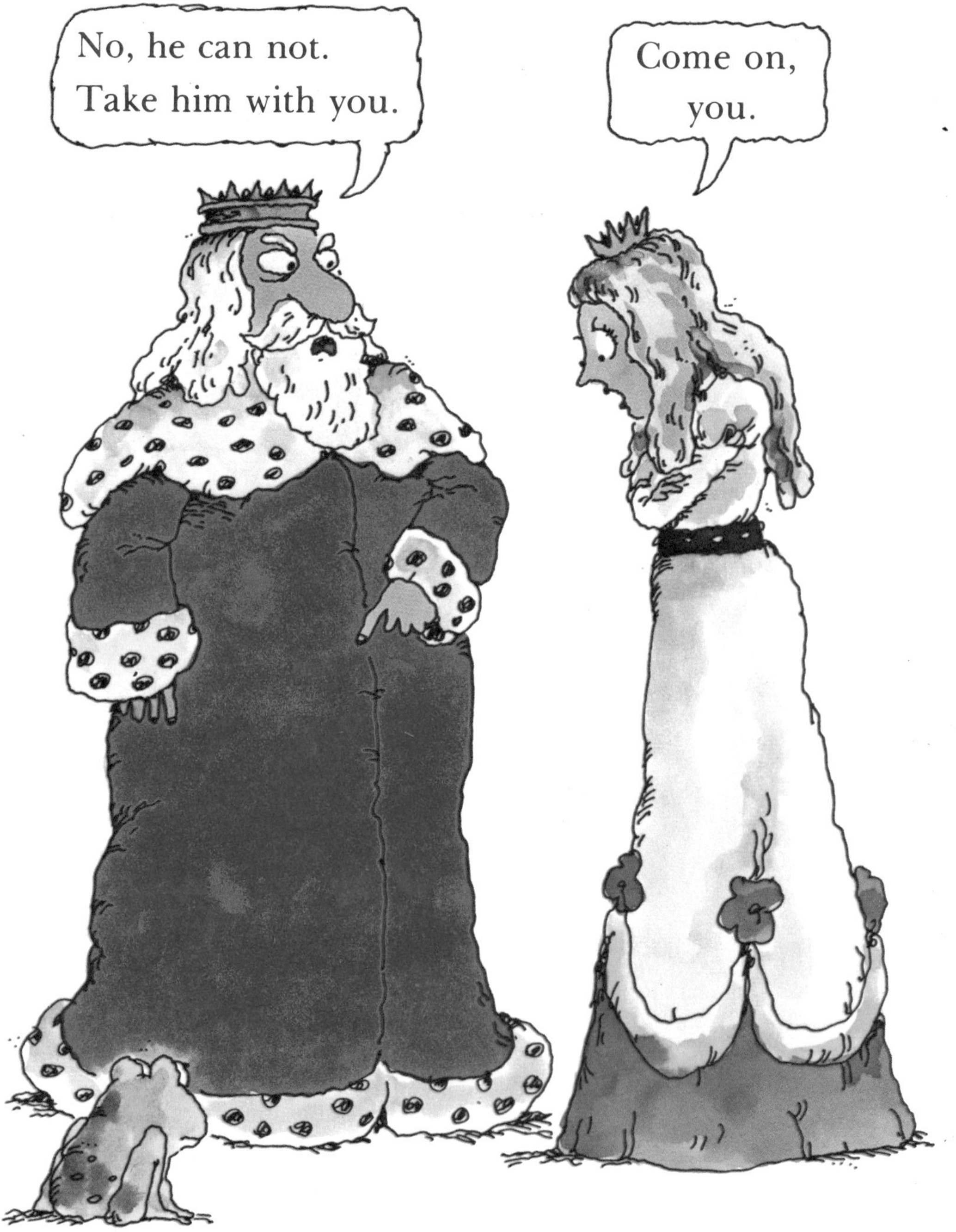
No, he can not.
Take him with you.
Come on,
you.

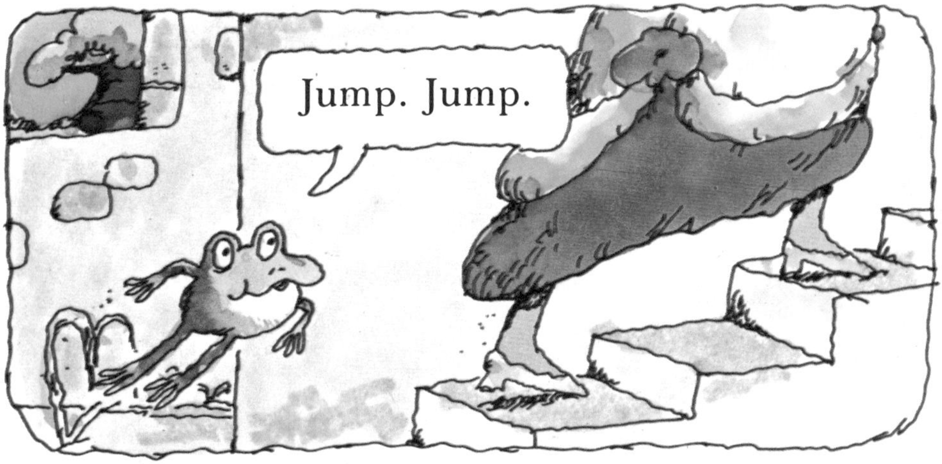
Jump. Jump.

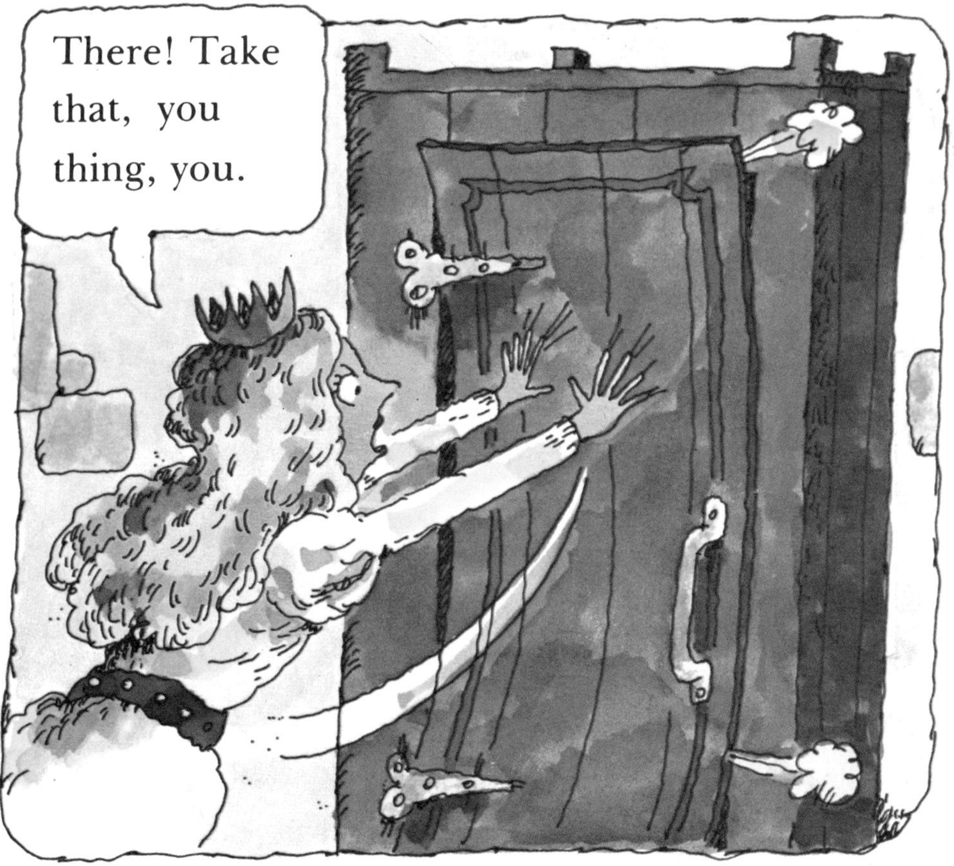
There! Take that, you thing, you.

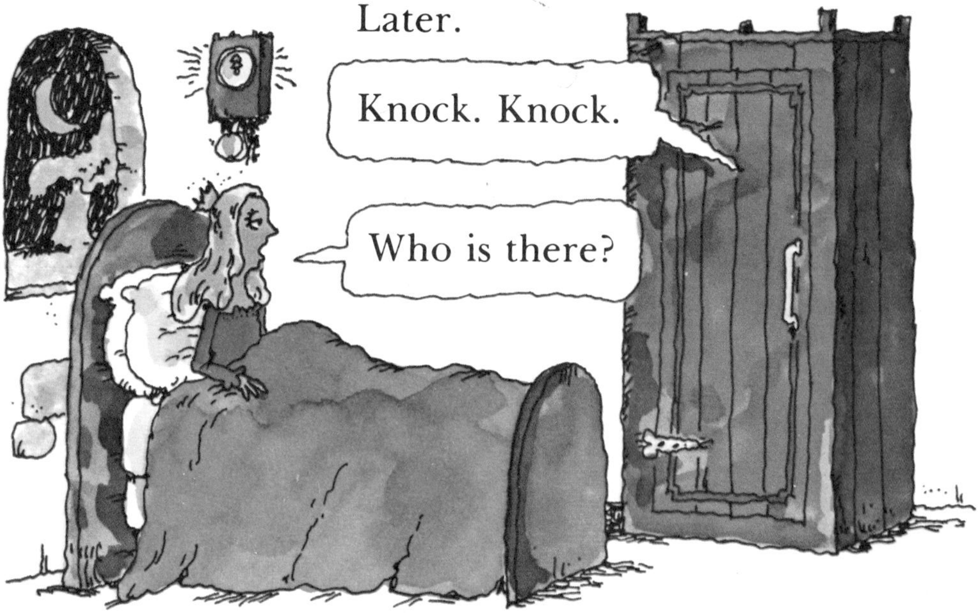
Later.
Knock. Knock.
Who is there?

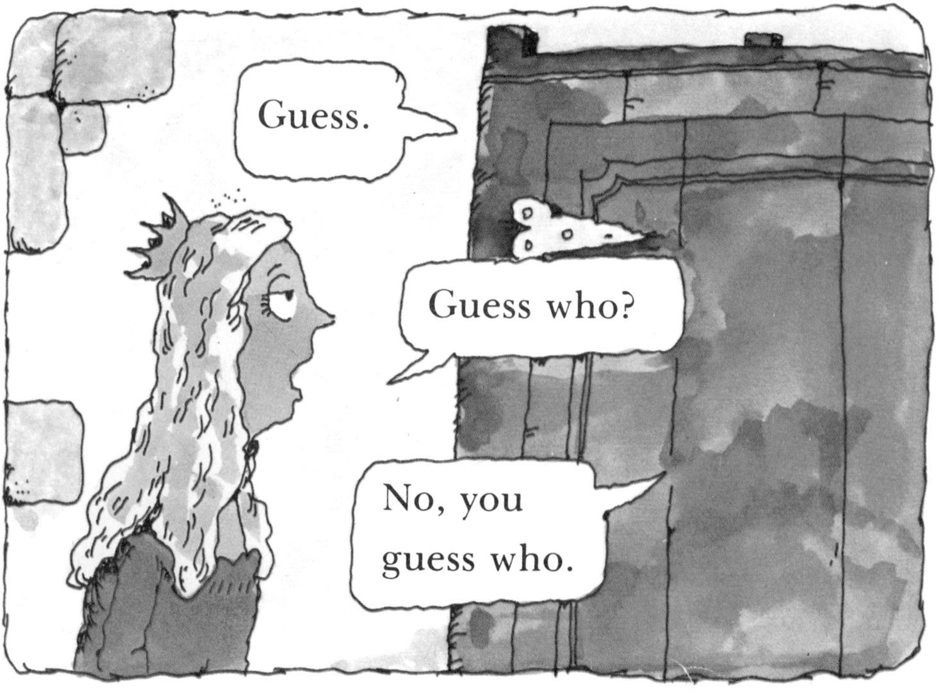
Guess.
Guess who?
No, you guess who.

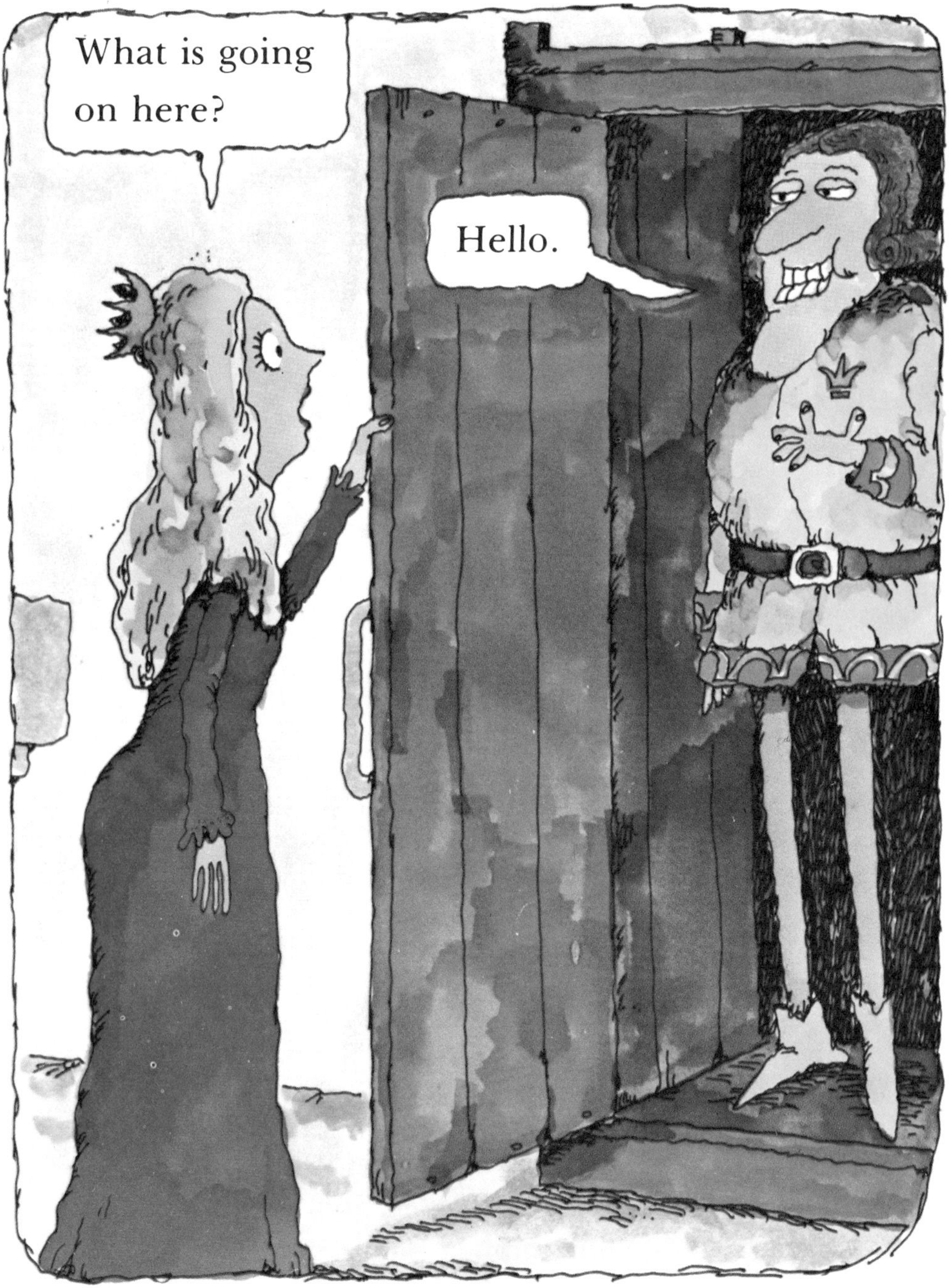
What is going on here?
Hello.

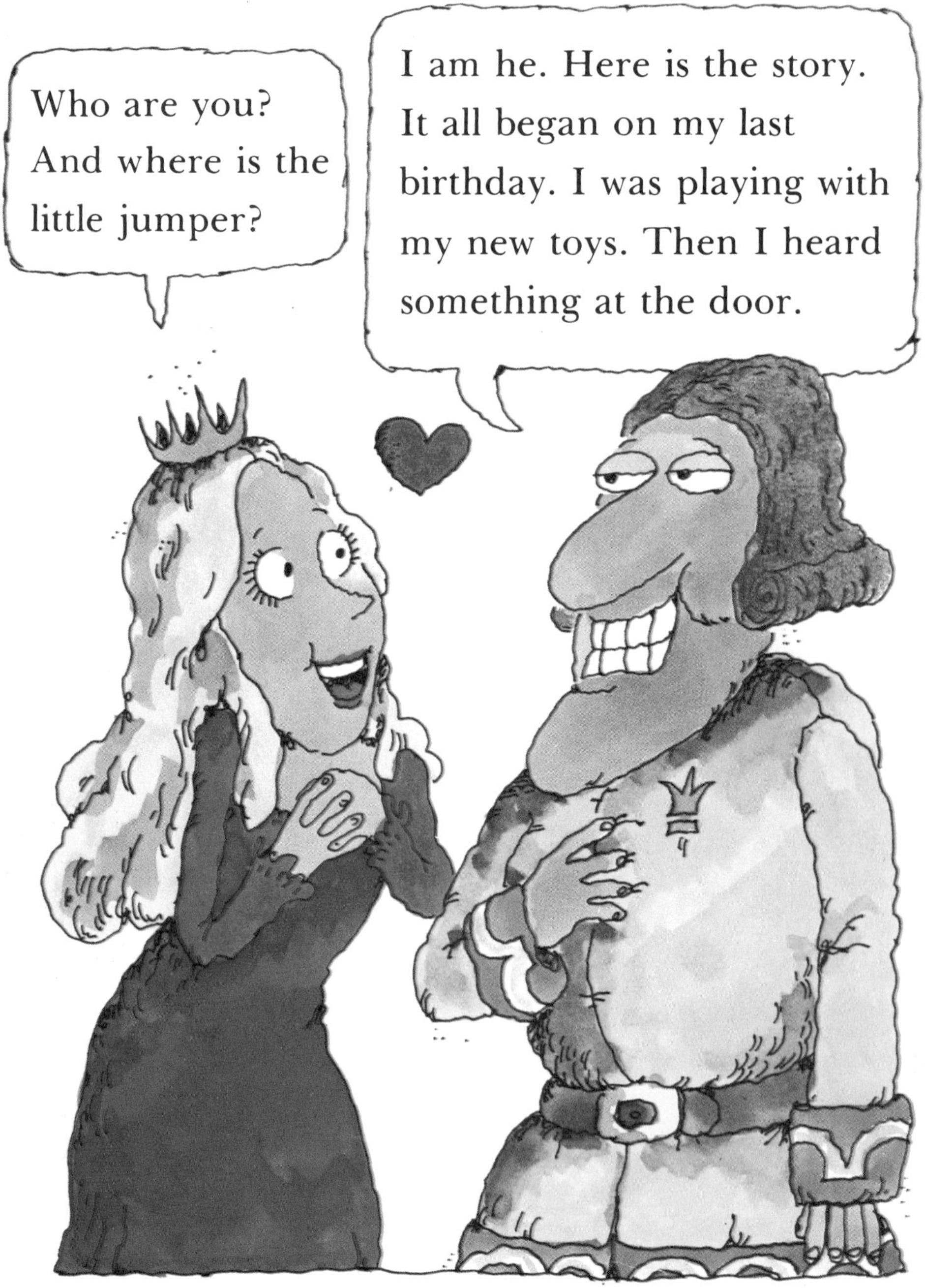
Who are you? And where is the little jumper?
I am he. Here is the story. It all began on my last birthday. I was playing with my new toys. Then I heard something at the door.

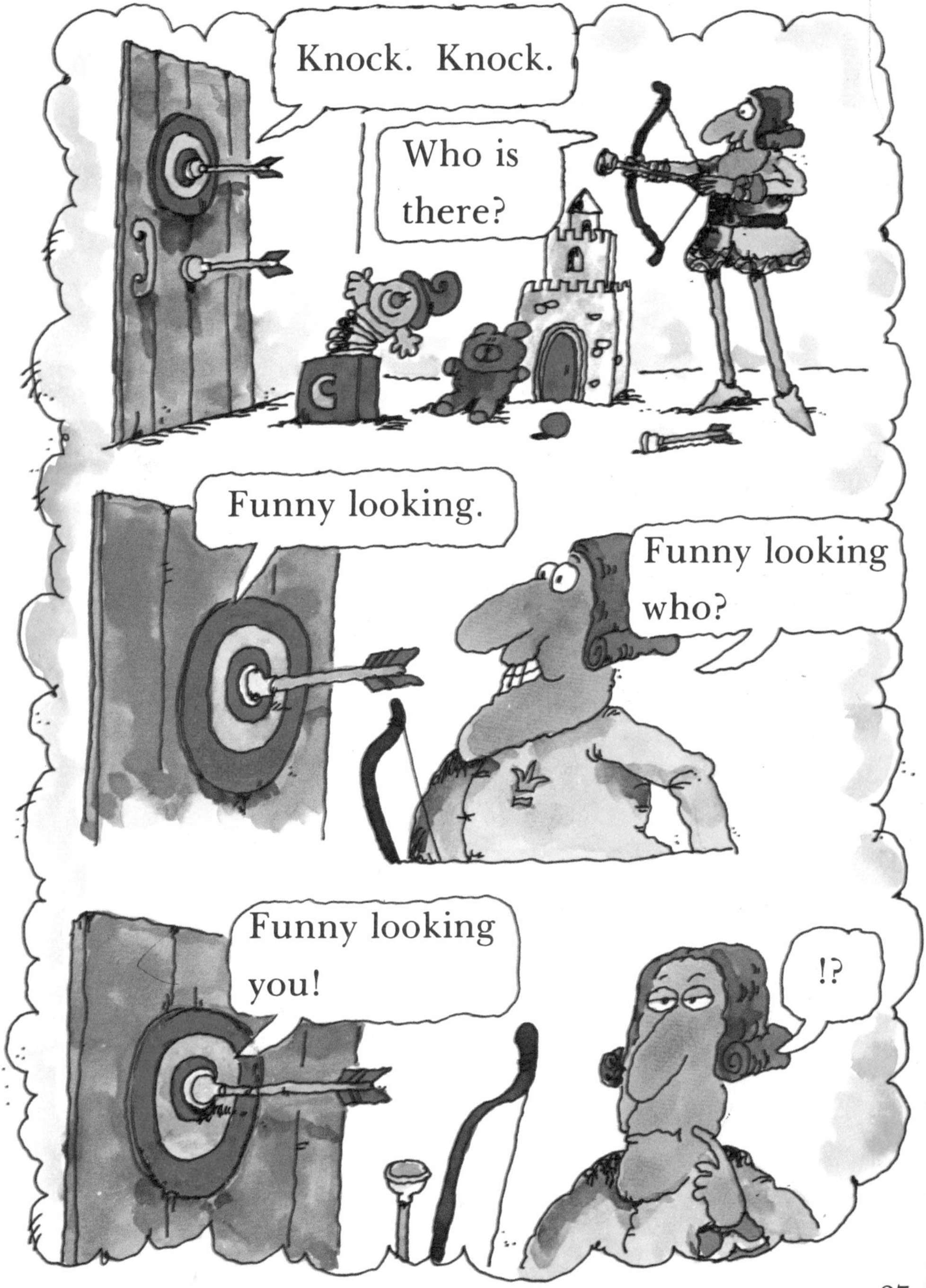
Knock. Knock.
Who is there?
Funny looking.
Funny looking who?
Funny looking you!
!?

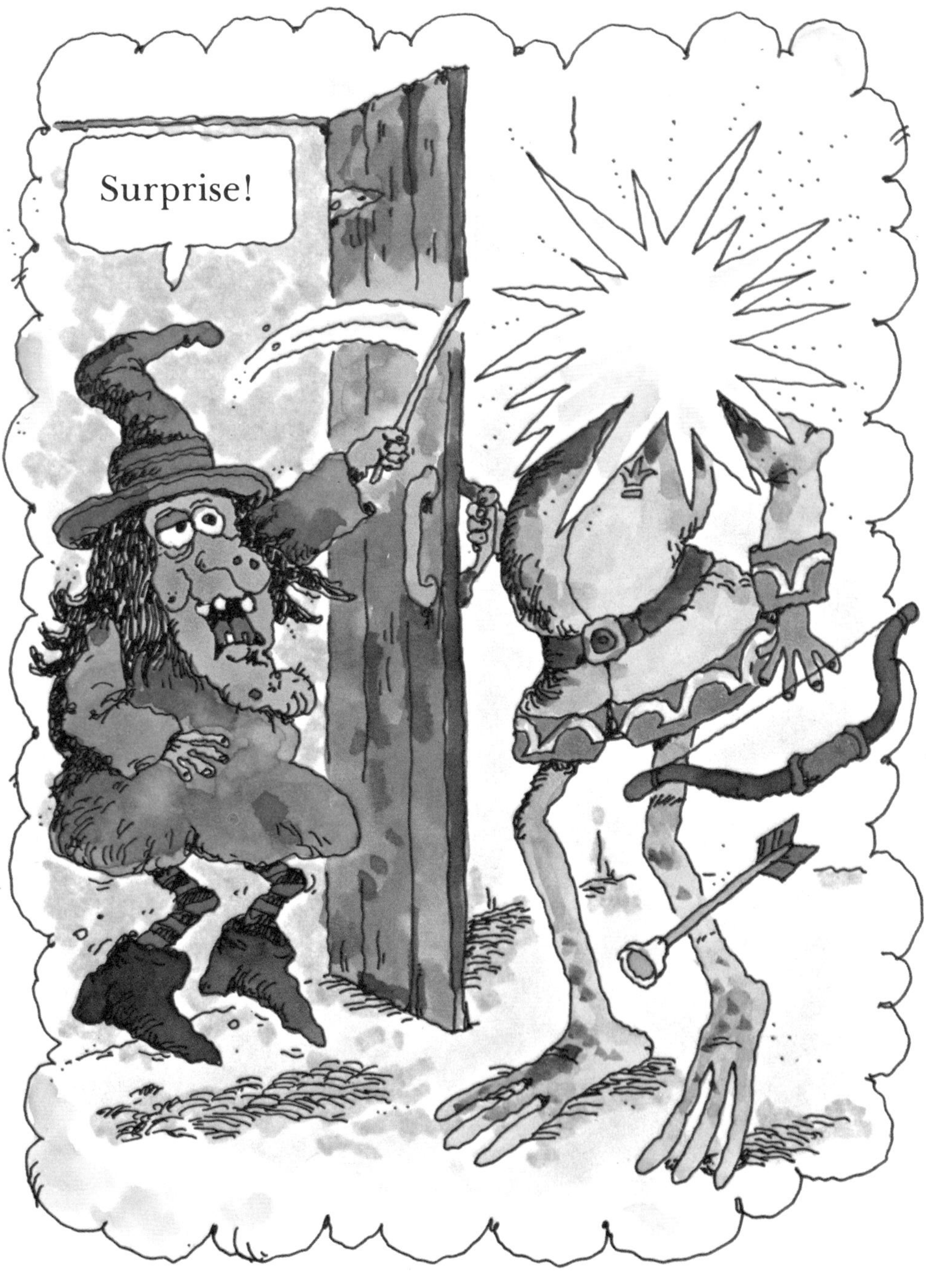
Surprise!

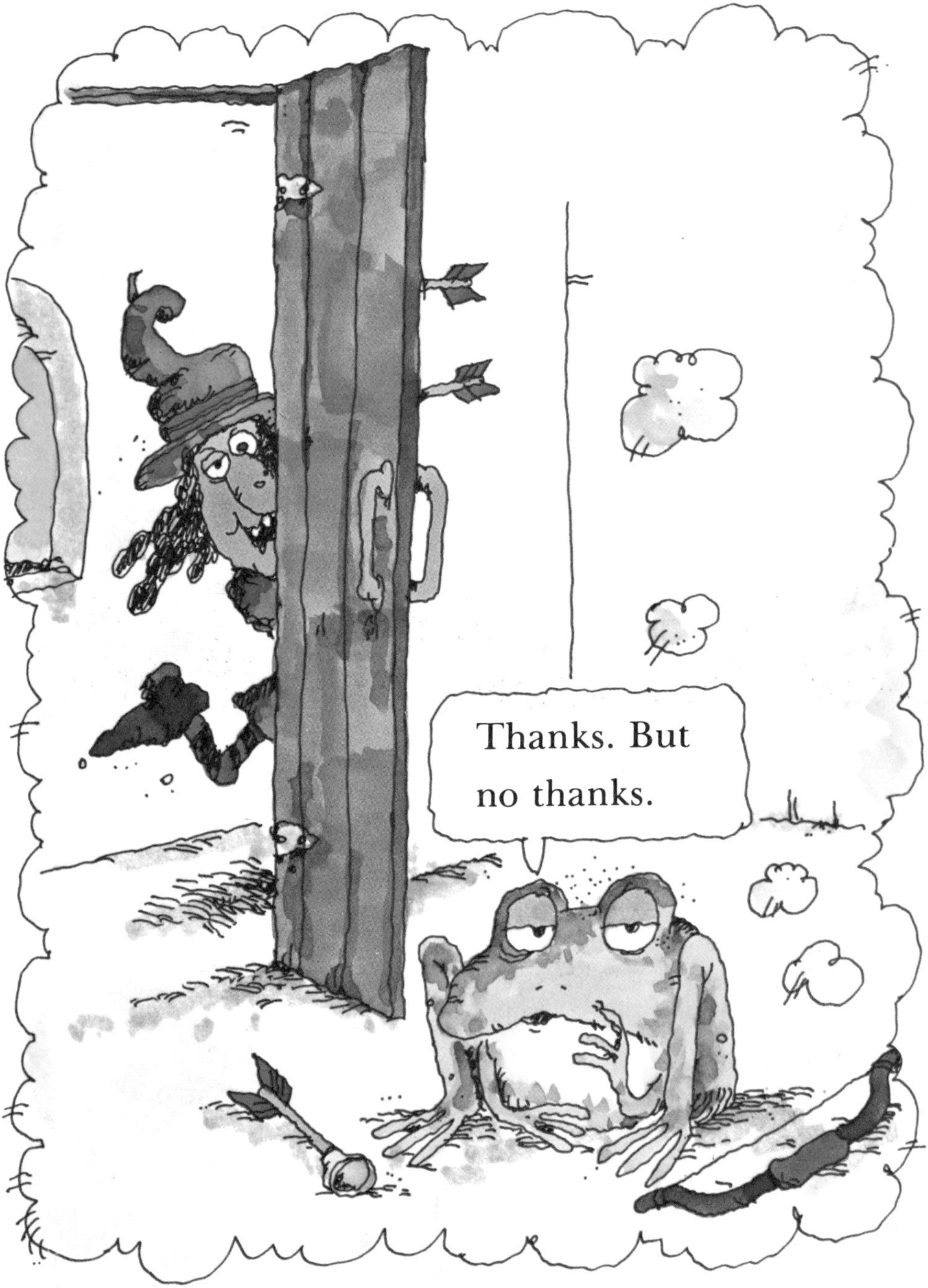
Thanks. But
no thanks.

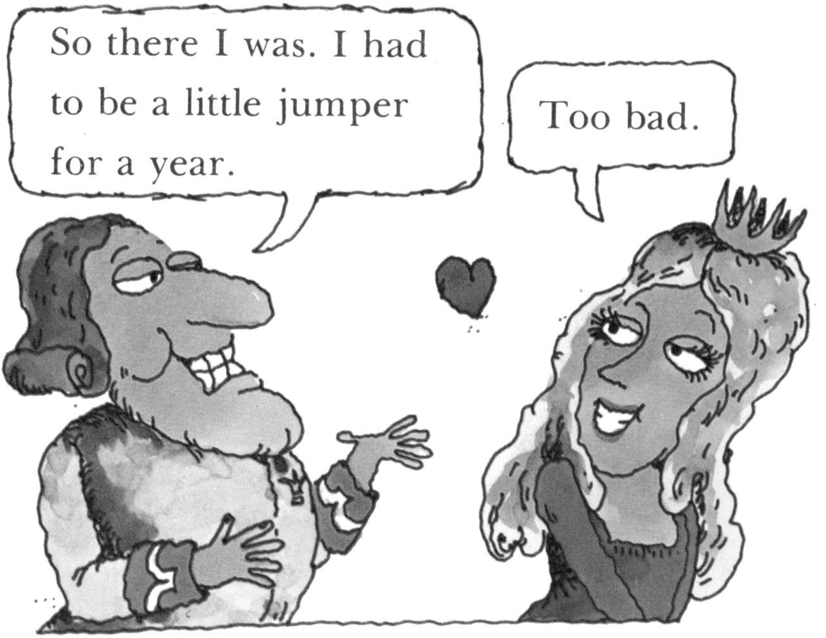
So there I was. I had to be a little jumper for a year.
Too bad.

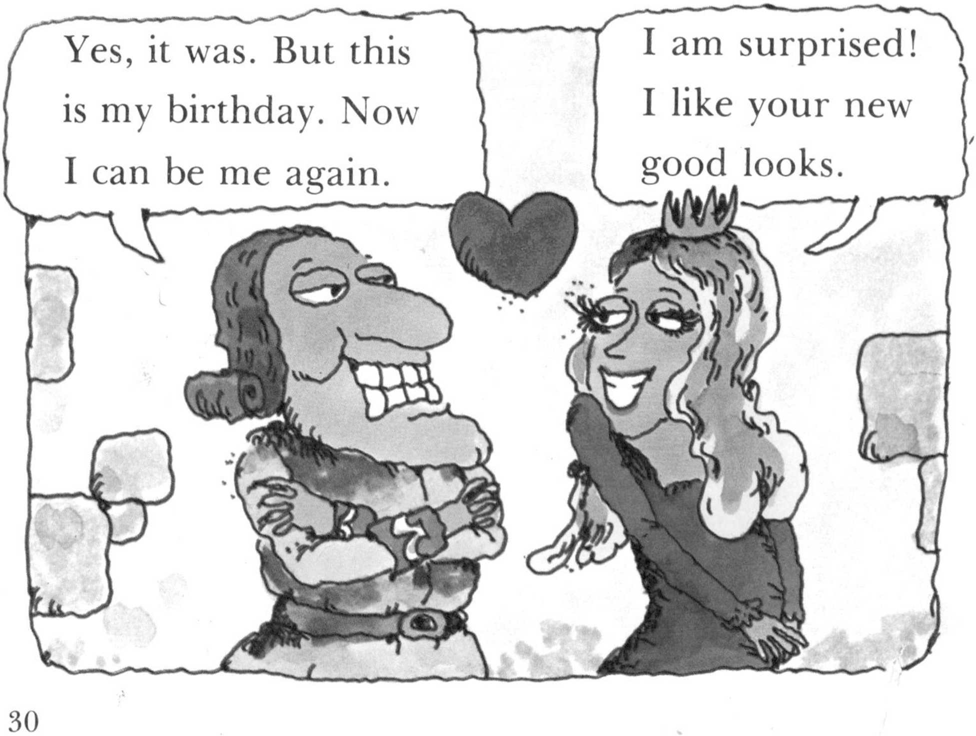
Yes, it was. But this is my birthday. Now I can be me again.
I am surprised! I like your new good looks.

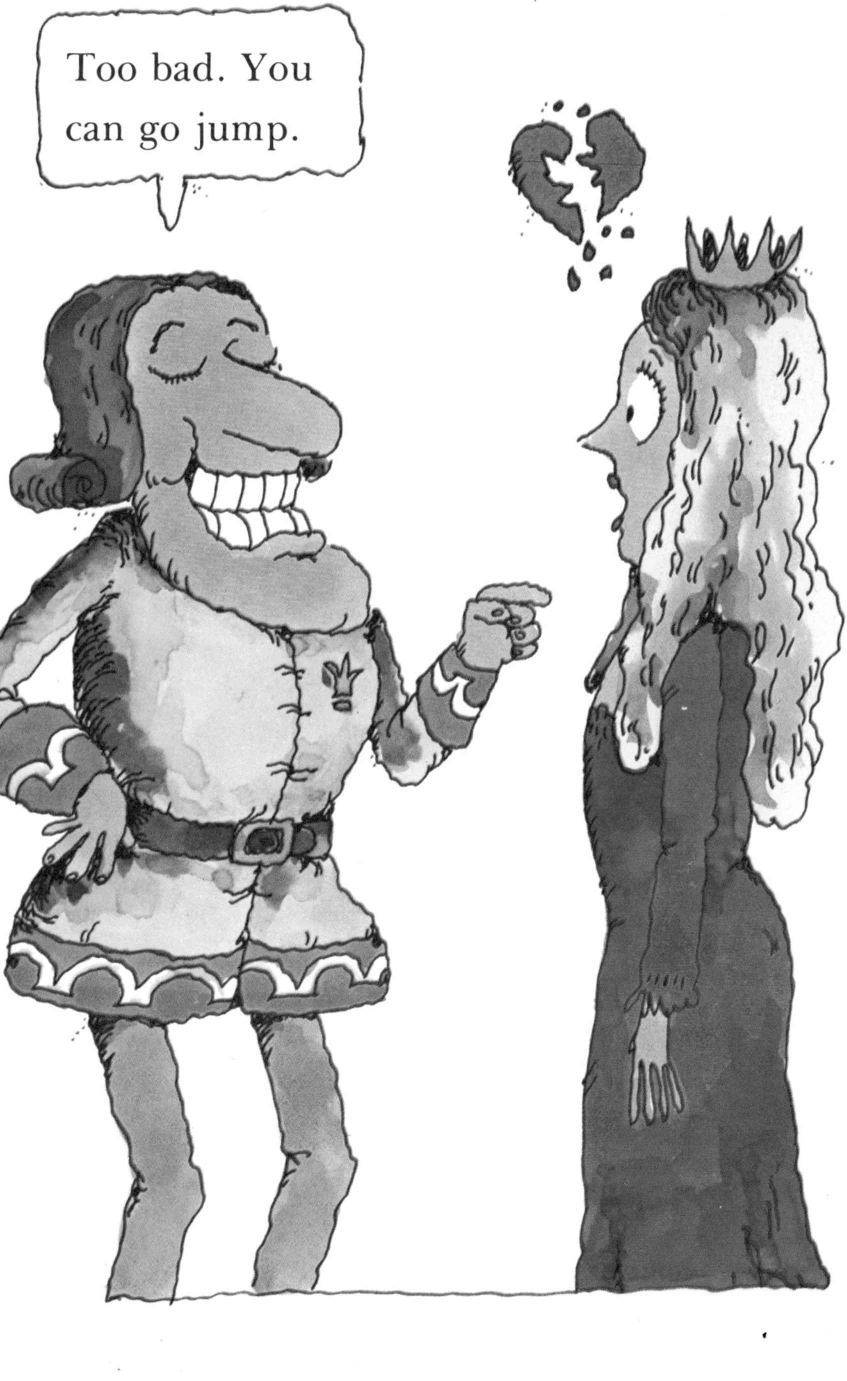
Too bad. You can go jump.

You Can Go Jump

Reading Level: Level One. *You Can Go Jump* employs a primary vocabulary of 94 words. It has been tested in first-grade classes, where it was read with ease.

Uses of This Book: Reading for fun, practice in appreciating characterization through humor. Children will enjoy this classic story, based on *The Frog Prince,* that they can read themselves.

Word List: All of the 94 words used in *You Can Go Jump* are listed. Regular plurals and verb forms of words already on the list are not listed separately, but the endings are given in parentheses after the word.

1	you		ball		am		in
	can		will		long	20	again
	go(ing)		give	12	stop	21	him
	jump(er)		me	13	at	23	that
4	what	7	want		the		thing
	see		have		big	24	later
	is		this		house		guess
	get		thank(s)		father	26	where
	oh		but		little		it
	yes	8	not		one		began
	no		be		eat		last
	help(ed)		funny	14	she		birthday
5	hello	9	to		away		was
	there		take	15	did		play(ing)
	good		home		a		new
	look(ing, s)		with		day		toys
	come		your(s)		too		then
	on		pet		bad		heard
6	so		say	16	knock		something
	I		he		who		door
	do	10	and		soon	28	surprise(d)
	for	11	here		out	29	year
	find		are	18	said		
	my		now	19	like		